CW00847248

EASY

COOKBOOK

THE EFFORTLESS CHEF SERIES

By
Chef Maggie Chow
Copyright © 2015 by Saxonberg
Associates

Published by
BookSumo, a division of Saxonberg
Associates
http://www.booksumo.com/

STAY TO THE END OF THE COOKBOOK AND RECEIVE....

I really appreciate when people, take the time to read all of my recipes.

So, as a gift for reading this entire cookbook you will receive a **massive collection of special recipes.**

Read to the end of and get my *Easy Specialty Cookbook Box Set for FREE*!

This box set includes the following:

1. ***Easy Sushi Cookbook***
2. ***Easy Dump Dinner Cookbook***
3. ***Easy Beans Cookbook***

Remember this box set is about **EASY** cooking.

In the ***Easy Sushi Cookbook*** you will learn the easiest methods to prepare almost every type of Japanese Sushi i.e. *California Rolls, the Perfect Sushi Rice, Crab Rolls, Osaka Style Sushi*, and so many others.

Then we go on to *Dump Dinners*. Nothing can be easier than a Dump Dinner. In the ***Easy Dump Dinner Cookbook*** we will learn how to master our slow cookers and make some amazingly unique dinners that will take almost ***no effort***.

Finally in the ***Easy Beans Cookbook*** we tackle one of my favorite side dishes: Beans. There are so many delicious ways to make Baked Beans and Bean Salads that I had to share them.

So stay till the end and then keep on cooking with my *Easy Specialty Cookbook Box Set*!

ABOUT THE AUTHOR.

Maggie Chow is the author and creator of your favorite *Easy Cookbooks* and *The Effortless Chef Series*. Maggie is a lover of all things related to food. Maggie loves nothing more than finding new recipes, trying them out, and then making them her own, by adding or removing ingredients, tweaking cooking times, and anything to make the recipe not only taste better, but be easier to cook!

For a complete listing of all my books please see my author page.

INTRODUCTION

Welcome to *The Effortless Chef Series*!
Thank you for taking the time to
download the *Easy Leeks Cookbook*.
Come take a journey with me into the
delights of easy cooking. The point of
this cookbook and all my cookbooks is to
exemplify the effortless nature of
cooking simply.

In this book we focus on Leeks. You will
find that even though the recipes are
simple, the taste of the dishes is quite
amazing.

So will you join me in an adventure of
simple cooking? If the answer is yes
(and I hope it is) please consult the table
of contents to find the dishes you are
most interested in. Once you are ready
jump right in and start cooking.

— Chef Maggie Chow

TABLE OF CONTENTS

ANY ISSUES? CONTACT ME

If you find that something important to you is missing from this book please contact me at maggie@booksumo.com.

I will try my best to re-publish a revised copy taking your feedback into consideration and let you know when the book has been revised with you in mind.

:)

— Chef Maggie Chow

LEGAL NOTES

COMMON ABBREVIATIONS

cup(s)	C.
tablespoon	tbsp
teaspoon	tsp
ounce	oz.
pound	lb

*All units used are standard American measurements

CHAPTER 1: EASY LEEKS RECIPES

OVEN ROASTED LEEKS

Ingredients

- 2 tbsps butter
- 1/4 C. all-purpose flour
- 1 1/2 C. skim milk
- 1/2 C. shredded Cheddar cheese
- 1/2 tsp garlic powder
- salt and pepper, to taste
- 4 medium leeks, halved lengthwise

Directions

- Coat a casserole dish with nonstick spray and then set your oven to 400 degrees before doing anything else.

- Combine the flour and butter until melted then slowly add in cheese and milk and continue heating and stirring until all the cheese is melted and everything is smooth.
- Now add in your pepper, garlic powder, and salt then shut the heat.
- Create a layer of leeks in your casserole dish and top it with the cheese mix.
- Cook everything in the oven for 35 mins. Then let it sit for 10 mins then serve.
- Enjoy.

Amount per serving (4 total)

Timing Information:

Preparation	20 m
Cooking	30 m
Total Time	50 m

Nutritional Information:

Calories	223 kcal
Fat	10.9 g
Carbohydrates	23.5g
Protein	8.9 g
Cholesterol	32 mg
Sodium	282 mg

* Percent Daily Values are based on a 2,000 calorie diet.

MAGGIE'S EASY VICHYSSOISE

Ingredients

- 1 tbsp butter
- 3 leeks, bulb only, sliced into rings
- 1 onion, sliced
- 5 potatoes, peeled and thinly sliced
- salt and pepper to taste
- 1/4 tsp dried thyme
- 1/2 tsp dried marjoram
- 1 bay leaf
- 5 C. chicken broth
- 1/4 C. heavy whipping cream

Directions

- Stir fry, for 12 mins, your onions and leeks, in butter. Then add your potatoes and the following seasonings: bay leaf, salt, marjoram, pepper, and thyme.

- Place a lid on the pot and let the contents cook for 10 more mins.
- Pour in the stock and get everything boiling.
- Once the mix is boiling set the heat to low and let the contents lightly cook for 32 mins.
- Get your blender and with a batch process, puree the soup, or use an immersion blender if you have one handy.
- When serving the dish add a dollop of fresh cream.
- Enjoy.

Amount per serving (4 total)

Timing Information:

Preparation	10 m
Cooking	50 m
Total Time	1 h

Nutritional Information:

Calories	353 kcal
Fat	9.5 g
Carbohydrates	60.3g
Protein	8.3 g
Cholesterol	34 mg
Sodium	1257 mg

* Percent Daily Values are based on a 2,000 calorie diet.

Buttery Leek Soup

Ingredients

- 1 C. butter
- 2 leeks, sliced
- salt and pepper to taste
- 1 quart chicken broth
- 1 tbsp cornstarch
- 4 C. Yukon Gold potatoes, peeled and diced
- 2 C. heavy cream

Directions

- Fry your leeks in butter and top them with some pepper and salt.
- Cook the veggies for 17 mins.
- Now add your broth to the mix and also cornstarch.
- Mix everything until smooth then add the Yukon and get the contents boiling.

- Add in some more pepper and salt.
- Once the soup is boiling lower the heat to a low level and let the soup gently cook uncovered for 35 mins.
- After serving the dish add some salt.
- Enjoy.

Amount per serving (8 total)

Timing Information:

Preparation	15 m
Cooking	1 h
Total Time	1 h 15 m

Nutritional Information:

Calories	488 kcal
Fat	45.4 g
Carbohydrates	18.7g
Protein	3.7 g
Cholesterol	145 mg
Sodium	673 mg

* Percent Daily Values are based on a 2,000 calorie diet.

CAULIFLOWER SOUP

Ingredients

- 2 tbsps olive oil
- 3 tbsps butter
- 3 leeks, cut into 1 inch pieces
- 1 large head cauliflower, diced
- 3 cloves garlic, finely diced
- 8 C. vegetable broth
- salt and freshly ground black pepper to taste
- 1 C. heavy cream (optional)

Directions

- Stir fry your cauliflower, leeks, and garlic in butter and olive oil for 12 mins. Then pour in your broth and get everything boiling.
- Once the mix is boiling place a lid on the pot, set the heat to low, and let the contents gently cook for 50 mins.

- Grab an immersion blender and puree the soup.
- If you do not have an immersion blender use a batch process to ladle all of soup into a blender.
- Blend the soup then pour it into a new pot.
- Add some more pepper and salt once the soup has been pureed and some cream and stir the contents.
- Enjoy warm.

Amount per serving (12 total)

Timing Information:

Preparation	15 m
Cooking	1 h
Total Time	1 h 15 m

Nutritional Information:

Calories	155 kcal
Fat	13.1 g
Carbohydrates	8.3g
Protein	2.4 g
Cholesterol	35 mg
Sodium	346 mg

* Percent Daily Values are based on a 2,000 calorie diet.

SOUTHERN FRENCH QUICHE

Ingredients

- 1 (9 inch) refrigerated pie crust
- 2 tsps butter
- 3 leeks, diced
- 1 pinch salt and black pepper to taste
- 1 C. light cream
- 1 1/4 C. shredded Gruyere cheese

Directions

- Set your oven to 375 degrees before doing anything else.
- Sauté your leeks in butter for 12 mins then add some pepper and salt.
- Set the heat to low and add in the cheese and cream.
- Stir the mix to get it smooth then fill your pie with the mixture.

- Cook the pie in the oven for 32 mins then let it rest on a countertop for 15 mins before serving.
- Enjoy.

Amount per serving (6 total)

Timing Information:

Preparation	10 m
Cooking	40 m
Total Time	1 h

Nutritional Information:

Calories	365 kcal
Fat	26.8 g
Carbohydrates	20.7g
Protein	11.2 g
Cholesterol	57 mg
Sodium	300 mg

* Percent Daily Values are based on a 2,000 calorie diet.

LEMON ARBORIO RISOTTO

Ingredients

- 2 tbsps olive oil
- 1 large leek, cleaned and thinly sliced
- 2 cloves garlic, minced
- 1 C. Arborio rice
- 2 C. low-sodium chicken broth, divided
- 1 C. dry white wine
- 1/2 lb bay scallops
- 1/2 lb medium shrimp, peeled and deveined
- 1 C. fresh snow peas, trimmed and halved crosswise
- 1 medium red bell pepper, diced
- 3 tbsps grated Parmesan cheese
- 2 tsps dried basil
- 2 tbsps lemon juice
- ground black pepper to taste

Directions

- Sauté your garlic and leeks in olive oil for 7 mins then add in your rice and cook the mix for 7 more mins.
- Make sure to constantly stir everything during this time.
- Now add 1.5 C. of broth and get it all boiling.
- Once the mix is boiling lower the heat and let it gently cook for 7 mins.
- Now add the rest of the broth and your wine and turn up the heat.
- Let everything cook for 4 mins with increased heat while stirring.
- Combine in: red pepper, scallops, peas, and shrimp.
- Cook the mix for about 6 more mins until the liquid is mostly evaporated.
- Now add: pepper, parmesan, lemon juice, and basil.
- Enjoy.

Amount per serving (6 total)

Timing Information:

Preparation	30 m
Cooking	25 m
Total Time	55 m

Nutritional Information:

Calories	330 kcal
Fat	6.5 g
Carbohydrates	39.6g
Protein	19.7 g
Cholesterol	74 mg
Sodium	201 mg

* Percent Daily Values are based on a 2,000 calorie diet.

BACON AU GRATIN

Ingredients

- 4 slices bacon, diced
- 1 leek, sliced
- 8 purple potatoes, thinly sliced
- 3 tbsps all-purpose flour
- 1/2 C. milk
- 6 oz. crumbled goat cheese
- 3/4 C. grated Parmesan cheese

Directions

- Set your oven to 400 degrees before doing anything else.
- Get a bowl, combine: flour and potatoes.
- Fry your bacon in a big pot and then add in your leeks and cook until they are soft.
- Add in your potatoes and add the cheese and milk. Continue stir frying until all the cheese is

melted then enter everything into a casserole dish.

- Garnish the casserole with parmesan and cook the contents for 47 mins in the oven.
- Enjoy.

Amount per serving (4 total)

Timing Information:

Preparation	15 m
Cooking	1 h
Total Time	1 h 15 m

Nutritional Information:

Calories	627 kcal
Fat	31.4 g
Carbohydrates	61.6g
Protein	27.4 g
Cholesterol	72 mg
Sodium	754 mg

* Percent Daily Values are based on a 2,000 calorie diet.

COUNTRYSIDE CRANBERRY STUFFING

Ingredients

- 12 C. white bread cubes
- 1 lb sweet Italian sausage, casings removed
- 1/4 C. butter
- 6 C. coarsely diced leeks
- 2 tart green apples - peeled, cored and diced
- 2 C. diced celery
- 4 tsps poultry seasoning
- 2 tsps dried rosemary, diced
- 1 C. dried cranberries
- 1 1/3 C. chicken broth
- salt and pepper to taste

Directions

- Set your oven to 350 degrees before doing anything else

- Layer your bread pieces in two different casserole or baking dishes and cook everything for 16 mins in the oven.
- Stir fry your sausage for 12 mins then remove the excess oils and place the meat to the side.
- Now stir fry your celery, leeks and apples, in butter, in the same pot, for 12 mins, then add in your poultry seasoning, and mix everything evenly.
- Now add the berries and rosemary.
- Stir the mix again to combine the spice and fruit.
- Combine the leeks with the toasted bread pieces and sausage in a big bowl and slowly add some broth into the mix to get everything slightly wet.
- Now add some pepper and salt.
- Pour the stuffing into a casserole dish and cook it in the oven for 47 mins with a covering of foil and 5 more mins with no cover.
- Enjoy.

Amount per serving (12 total)

Timing Information:

Preparation	35 m
Cooking	1 h
Total Time	1 h 35 m

Nutritional Information:

Calories	359 kcal
Fat	17.5 g
Carbohydrates	41.5g
Protein	9.9 g
Cholesterol	39 mg
Sodium	839 mg

* Percent Daily Values are based on a 2,000 calorie diet.

IRISH POTATOES

Ingredients

- 1 lb cabbage
- 1 lb potatoes
- 2 leeks
- 1 C. milk
- salt and pepper to taste
- 1 pinch ground mace
- 1/2 C. butter

Directions

- Cook your cabbage in boiling water until soft. Then let it cool.
- Once the cabbage has cooled begin to blend it.
- Now cook your potatoes in boiling water until soft and remove all the liquid and mash them.
- Dice up your leeks and cook them in simmering milk until tender.

- Once the leeks are soft add the entire mix to the mashed potatoes and mash everything together again.
- Finally add in your cabbage to the mix and mash the contents one more time.
- Enter everything into a big pot and warm it up again before serving the dish with melted butter.
- Enjoy.

Amount per serving (5 total)

Timing Information:

Preparation	10 m
Cooking	30 m
Total Time	50 m

Nutritional Information:

Calories	302 kcal
Fat	19.7 g
Carbohydrates	28.6g
Protein	5.3 g
Cholesterol	53 mg
Sodium	180 mg

* Percent Daily Values are based on a 2,000 calorie diet.

MAGGIE'S EASY SPLIT PEA SOUP

Ingredients

- 6 slices bacon, cut into 1 inch pieces
- 1 small onion, diced
- 1 leek, thinly sliced
- 1 large carrot, diced
- 2 cloves garlic, minced
- 4 (10.5 oz.) cans chicken broth
- 1 1/2 C. green split peas
- 2 bay leaves
- 1 tsp diced fresh rosemary

Directions

- Fry your bacon, in a saucepan, then add in: garlic, onions, carrots, and leeks.
- Cook everything for 10 mins. Then add the broth: rosemary, split peas, and bay leaves.

- Get everything boiling, place a lid on the pot, set the heat to low and let the contents gently cook for 1 hour.
- Make sure you stir the soup every 10 to 15 mins.
- Enjoy.

Amount per serving (6 total)

Timing Information:

Preparation	20 m
Cooking	1 h 15 m
Total Time	1 h 35 m

Nutritional Information:

Calories	253 kcal
Fat	5 g
Carbohydrates	35.5g
Protein	17 g
Cholesterol	15 mg
Sodium	1195 mg

* Percent Daily Values are based on a 2,000 calorie diet.

GREEN SOUP

Ingredients

- 2 tsps olive oil
- 4 leeks, bulb only, diced
- 2 cloves garlic, diced
- 2 (16 oz.) cans fat-free chicken broth
- 2 (16 oz.) cans cannellini beans, rinsed and drained
- 2 bay leaves
- 2 tsps ground cumin
- 1/2 C. whole wheat couscous
- 2 C. packed fresh spinach
- salt and pepper to taste

Directions

- Stir fry your garlic and leeks in olive oil for 7 mins then add: cumin, broth, bay leaves, beans.
- Get everything boiling, lower the heat, and pour in your couscous.

- Place a lid on the pot and let the couscous gently boil for 6 mins then add your pepper, salt, and spinach.
- Enjoy hot.

Amount per serving (8 total)

Timing Information:

Preparation	10 m
Cooking	15 m
Total Time	25 m

Nutritional Information:

Calories	179 kcal
Fat	2 g
Carbohydrates	30.6g
Protein	9.4 g
Cholesterol	0 mg
Sodium	432 mg

* Percent Daily Values are based on a 2,000 calorie diet.

MUSTARD AND CHEESE YUKON SOUP

Ingredients

- 2 leeks, finely diced (white part only)
- 1 clove garlic, finely diced
- 4 medium potatoes (red or Yukon Gold), diced
- 2 tbsps butter, divided
- 1 tbsp olive oil
- 1 1/2 tsps ground mustard
- 2 tbsps flour
- 1/2 C. water
- 3 C. chicken broth
- salt, pepper, and celery salt, to taste
- 1/2 C. shredded Cheddar cheese
- 2 tbsps Parmesan cheese
- 1 C. milk
- 3 oz. diced portobello mushrooms
- croutons for garnish, if desired

Directions

- Get a bowl, combine: flour, mustard, celery salt, regular salt, and pepper.
- Now add in the broth and water and mix everything.
- Cook: potatoes, garlic, and leeks in half of your butter and olive oil with a low level of heat until you find that the potatoes are tender.
- Stir the contents often while they cook to avoid burning.
- Once the potatoes are soft add in your broth mix.
- Get the broth and potatoes boiling, lower the heat, and let it gently cook for 1 hr.
- While the broth is boiling cook your mushrooms in the rest of the butter and then add them to the potatoes once they are tender.
- Now mash your potatoes in the pot with a potato masher and then add in parmesan, cheddar, and milk.

- Let the cheese melt then serve the dish.
- Enjoy.

Amount per serving (6 total)

Timing Information:

Preparation	30 m
Cooking	1 h 15 m
Total Time	1 h 45 m

Nutritional Information:

Calories	289 kcal
Fat	12.2 g
Carbohydrates	37.3g
Protein	8.6 g
Cholesterol	25 mg
Sodium	909 mg

* Percent Daily Values are based on a 2,000 calorie diet.

Italian Tortellini Soup

Ingredients

- 1 tbsp olive oil
- 5 large mushrooms, diced
- 2 large leeks, cleaned, and cut into 1/4 inch thick rounds
- 6 C. chicken broth
- 4 chicken sausages, sliced in 1/3-inch rounds
- 1 (9 oz.) package cheese tortellini
- 3 cloves garlic, minced
- 3 tbsps hot pepper sauce (e.g. Tabasco(TM)), or to taste
- salt and pepper to taste
- 5 sprigs diced fresh cilantro, for garnish

Directions

- Stir fry your leeks and mushrooms in olive oil for 7

mins. Then place them to the side.

- Now a get a big pot, add in your broth, and get it boiling.
- Once everything is boiling add: hot sauce, sausage, garlic, and tortellini.
- Now lower the heat and pour in your mushrooms and leeks.
- Place a lid on the pot and let the contents gently boil for 35 mins.
- When serving your dish top it with some cilantro.
- Enjoy warm.

Amount per serving (6 total)

Timing Information:

Preparation	25 m
Cooking	35 m
Total Time	1 h

Nutritional Information:

Calories	313 kcal
Fat	13 g
Carbohydrates	30.8g
Protein	18.2 g
Cholesterol	66 mg
Sodium	890 mg

* Percent Daily Values are based on a 2,000 calorie diet.

WINTER SOUP

Ingredients

- 2 tbsps butter, or more if needed
- 2 leeks, cleaned and diced
- 1/2 C. diced scallions
- 6 potatoes, peeled and cubed
- 4 C. chicken broth
- 1 C. half-and-half
- 4 oz. shredded Monterey
- 4 oz. of pepper jack cheese
- 1 tbsp diced fresh parsley
- 1 tsp garlic powder
- salt and ground black pepper to taste

Directions

- Stir fry your scallions and leeks in butter for 7 mins then add in your broth and potatoes.
- Cook the mix for 27 mins until soft.

- Add your half and half and let the contents gently boil for 20 more mins.
- Add your Monterey and pepper jack cheese as well as: black pepper, parsley, salt, and garlic powder.
- Let the cheese completely melt for 7 more mins.
- Enjoy.

Amount per serving (6 total)

Timing Information:

Preparation	20 m
Cooking	45 m
Total Time	1 h 5 m

Nutritional Information:

Calories	362 kcal
Fat	15.4 g
Carbohydrates	45.7g
Protein	11.6 g
Cholesterol	48 mg
Sodium	886 mg

* Percent Daily Values are based on a 2,000 calorie diet.

CILANTRO SALMON SPAGHETTI

Ingredients

- 1/2 (8 oz.) package spaghetti
- 1 tbsp butter
- 1 large leek - light parts only, rinsed, and diced
- salt to taste
- 1/2 C. white wine
- 1/2 lemon, juiced
- 1 C. crème fraiche
- 1 tsp tarragon Dijon mustard
- 1 pinch cayenne pepper, or to taste
- 6 oz. skinless, boneless salmon, sliced
- 1/2 C. diced cilantro, or to taste
- 1 pinch cayenne pepper

Directions

- Boil your pasta in water and salt for 13 mins then remove all the liquid.
- Stir fry your leeks in butter for 8 mins then add in salt, lemon juice, and wine.
- Get everything boiling and let the contents gently cook for 7 mins until most of the liquid has cooked out.
- Now add your crème, cayenne, and mustard.
- Lower the heat and continue cooking the contents for 6 mins then add your fish and cook the fish for 4 more mins.
- Shut the heat and add the cilantro.
- Combine the salmon and sauce with the pasta and stir everything.
- When serving the dish add a bit more cayenne.
- Enjoy.

Amount per serving (2 total)

Timing Information:

Preparation	15 m
Cooking	30 m
Total Time	45 m

Nutritional Information:

Calories	896 kcal
Fat	56.7 g
Carbohydrates	62.2g
Protein	31.3 g
Cholesterol	216 mg
Sodium	401 mg

* Percent Daily Values are based on a 2,000 calorie diet.

STIR FRIED LEEKS

Ingredients

- 2 leeks, finely diced
- 4 carrots, finely diced
- 1/3 C. chicken broth
- 2 tbsps butter
- 1 tbsp white sugar
- 1/2 tsp dried thyme
- 1/2 tsp kosher salt
- 1/8 tsp ground black pepper

Directions

- Boil the following in a big pot: pepper, leeks, salt, carrots, thyme, broth, sugar, and butter.
- Once everything is boiling lower the heat and let the mix gently cook for 17 mins, until most of the liquid has cooked out.
- Continue cooking everything for another 4 to 5 mins until the

veggies are a bit brown then
serve.
- Enjoy.

Amount per serving (6 total)

Timing Information:

Preparation	15 m
Cooking	20 m
Total Time	35 m

Nutritional Information:

Calories	78 kcal
Fat	4.1 g
Carbohydrates	10.3g
Protein	0.9 g
Cholesterol	10 mg
Sodium	275 mg

* Percent Daily Values are based on a 2,000 calorie diet.

PRIMAVERA

Ingredients

- 1 bunch fresh basil
- 3 C. chicken broth, divided
- 1/2 C. olive oil
- 2 cloves garlic
- 1 lb fettuccine pasta
- 2 tbsps olive oil
- 1 large leek, white and light green parts only, diced
- 1 bunch green onions, diced
- 2 jalapeno peppers, seeded and diced
- 2 pinches salt
- 2 zucchinis, diced
- 1 C. diced sugar snap peas
- 1/2 C. shelled English peas
- 1 bunch asparagus, stalks diced, tips left whole
- 1/2 C. grated Parmesan cheese, or as needed

Directions

- Blanch your basil for a few secs and place them in cold water for 3 mins.
- Separate the leaves from the stems and place them to the side.
- Blend: garlic, basil, half a C. of olive oil, and 1 C. of broth.
- Now begin to boil your pasta with the water that blanched the basil for 9 mins. Then remove all the liquid.
- Stir fry your leeks in 2 tbsps of olive oil for 7 mins. Then add: salt and jalapenos.
- Cook the mix for 4 more mins. Then turn up the heat and add 2 C. of broth and: English peas, snap peas, and zucchini.
- Let this boil for 6 mins. Then add in the asparagus and cook everything for 4 more mins.
- Add a quarter of basil sauce to the zucchini and cook the contents for 2 mins.

- Shut the heat and place your pasta in the pot.
- Stir everything and top the dish with parmesan.
- Now place a wrapping of foil over the pot and let the noodle soak up the liquid for 7 mins.
- Stir everything once more.
- Enjoy.

Amount per serving (6 total)

Timing Information:

Preparation	20 m
Cooking	20 m
Total Time	45 m

Nutritional Information:

Calories	589 kcal
Fat	26.9 g
Carbohydrates	72.5g
Protein	18.6 g
Cholesterol	8 mg
Sodium	607 mg

* Percent Daily Values are based on a 2,000 calorie diet.

SWISS AND ROMANO QUICHE

Ingredients

- 2 tbsps butter
- 2 C. sliced leeks
- 1 (9 inch) frozen pie crust, thawed
- 1 C. shredded Swiss cheese
- 1/4 C. grated Romano cheese
- 1 tbsp all-purpose flour
- 4 eggs
- 1 3/4 C. heavy cream
- 1 tomato, thinly sliced
- salt and pepper to taste

Directions

- Set your oven to 450 degrees before doing anything else.
- Get a bowl, mix: flour, Romano, and cheddar.
- Get a 2nd bowl, mix: cream, and whisked eggs.

- Stir fry your leeks in butter and layer them in a pie crust.
- Now top the leeks with the cheese mix then the cream mix.
- Add a final layer of tomato, pepper, and salt.
- Cook everything in the oven for 17 mins at 450 then for 32 mins at 325 degrees.
- Serve after letting the quiche sit for 10 mins.
- Enjoy.

Amount per serving (8 total)

Timing Information:

Preparation	15 m
Cooking	45 m
Total Time	1 h

Nutritional Information:

Calories	472 kcal
Fat	39.4 g
Carbohydrates	15.7g
Protein	14.9 g
Cholesterol	204 mg
Sodium	359 mg

* Percent Daily Values are based on a 2,000 calorie diet.

Autumn Pumpkin Soup

Ingredients

- 1 tbsp vegetable oil
- 1 onion, finely diced
- 1 leek, diced
- 1 lb peeled and diced pumpkin
- 3/4 lb sweet potato, peeled and cubed
- 1 quart vegetable broth
- 1 1/4 C. light coconut milk

Directions

- Stir fry your onions and leeks in oil until tender then add: broth, potatoes, and pumpkin.
- Get everything boiling, place a lid on the pan, set the heat to low, and let the contents gently cook for 17 mins.
- Now mash the veggies and add: pepper, coconut milk, and salt.

- Enjoy.

Amount per serving (8 total)

Timing Information:

Preparation	20 m
Cooking	25 m
Total Time	45 m

Nutritional Information:

Calories	130 kcal
Fat	5.4 g
Carbohydrates	18.4g
Protein	2.4 g
Cholesterol	0 mg
Sodium	261 mg

* Percent Daily Values are based on a
2,000 calorie diet.

A CASSEROLE FROM DEMARK

Ingredients

- 2 lbs potatoes, peeled and diced
- 1/4 C. milk
- 2 lbs leeks, diced
- 1 lb ground beef
- 1 onion, diced
- 1 red bell pepper, diced
- 1 green bell pepper, diced
- 1 tbsp finely diced green chile peppers
- soy sauce to taste
- 1 (8 oz.) package shredded Cheddar cheese
- 6 oz. cooked ham, cut into thin strips

Directions

- Set your oven to 350 degrees before doing anything else.

- Boil your potatoes in water and salt for 17 mins. Then remove the liquid and mash them with some milk.
- Simultaneously boil your leeks in water for 11 mins. Then remove the liquid as well.
- Stir fry your beef then add in: soy sauce, bell peppers, chili peppers, and onions.
- Cook everything for a few more mins until the entire mix is soft.
- Combine the following into a casserole dish: beef, potatoes, and leeks.
- Top the contents with some cheese, ham, and more cheese.
- Cook the dish in the oven for 27 mins.
- Enjoy.

Amount per serving (8 total)

Timing Information:

Preparation	25 m
Cooking	45 m
Total Time	1 h 10 m

Nutritional Information:

Calories	515 kcal
Fat	28.9 g
Carbohydrates	39.7g
Protein	25 g
Cholesterol	90 mg
Sodium	554 mg

* Percent Daily Values are based on a 2,000 calorie diet.

A Soup from Scotland

Ingredients

- 4 lbs chicken thighs, bone in, skin removed
- 10 C. water
- 1 onion, diced
- 1/3 C. barley
- 1 (10.5 oz.) can condensed chicken broth
- 7 leeks, sliced
- 2 stalks celery, thickly sliced
- 1 sprig fresh thyme, diced
- 1 tbsp diced fresh parsley
- 1 tsp salt
- 1/2 tsp ground black pepper

Directions

- Boil: barley, chicken, onions, and water.

- Once everything is boiling lower the heat and let the contents gently cook for 1 hr.
- Now take out the chicken and remove the skin and bones.
- Begin to dice the meat then place everything back into the pot.
- Combine in: pepper, broth, salt, leeks, parsley, celery, and thyme.
- Let the contents simmer for 35 mins.
- Enjoy.

Amount per serving (12 total)

Timing Information:

Preparation	10 m
Cooking	1 h 30 m
Total Time	1 h 40 m

Nutritional Information:

Calories	243 kcal
Fat	6.5 g
Carbohydrates	12.4g
Protein	32.4 g
Cholesterol	126 mg
Sodium	497 mg

* Percent Daily Values are based on a 2,000 calorie diet.

Sweet Salmon Stir Fry

Ingredients

- 4 leeks
- 2 tbsps butter
- 1 tbsp brown sugar
- 3 carrots, cut into matchsticks
- kosher salt to taste
- 2 lbs salmon fillets
- 2 tsps olive oil
- kosher salt and ground black pepper to taste

Directions

- Cover a casserole dish with foil and nonstick spray then set your oven to 425 degrees before doing anything else.
- Chop up your leeks removing the hard leaves, and the root.
- Now rinse the leeks under cold water and pat them dry.

- Stir fry the leeks in butter for 7 mins. Then add brown sugar and continue cooking for 17 more mins (low to medium heat stir in intervals of 4 mins).
- Add: salt and carrots.
- Cook everything for 7 more mins.
- Layer your salmon in the casserole dish and top the fish with olive oil, pepper, and salt.
- Cook the salmon in the oven for 9 to 12 mins for each side.
- Place everything on serving plates and evenly divide the leeks amongst our salmon servings.
- Enjoy.

Amount per serving (4 total)

Timing Information:

Preparation	15 m
Cooking	40 m
Total Time	55 m

Nutritional Information:

Calories	523 kcal
Fat	30.4 g
Carbohydrates	20.3g
Protein	41 g
Cholesterol	127 mg
Sodium	399 mg

* Percent Daily Values are based on a 2,000 calorie diet.

INDIAN APPLE SOUP

Ingredients

- 1 tbsp margarine
- 2 tsps curry powder
- 3 leeks, diced
- 3/4 C. diced potatoes
- 2 Granny Smith apples -- peeled, cored and diced
- 3 C. vegetable broth
- salt and pepper to taste
- 1/4 C. plain yogurt

Directions

- Stir fry your curry for 2 mins in butter and add the apples, leeks, and potatoes.
- Continue stirring and frying for 7 mins.
- Now add the broth and get everything boiling.

- Once the mix is boiling, place lid on the pot, set the heat to low, and let the contents gently cook for 22 mins.
- Grab an immersion blender and puree the soup. Or use a food processor and blend the soup in batches.
- If blending in batches place the resulting puree in a separate pot.
- Add your preferred amount of pepper and salt to the pureed soup and reheat everything before serving.
- Enjoy.

Amount per serving (4 total)

Timing Information:

Preparation	10 m
Cooking	26 m
Total Time	36 m

Nutritional Information:

Calories	133 kcal
Fat	3.6 g
Carbohydrates	23.9g
Protein	2.9 g
Cholesterol	< 1 mg
Sodium	< 395 mg

* Percent Daily Values are based on a 2,000 calorie diet.

GREEK LEMON AND LEEKS

Ingredients

- 1/4 C. extra-virgin olive oil
- 3 cloves garlic, finely diced
- 1 tbsp white sugar
- 2 lbs leeks, white parts only, finely diced
- 1 lemon, juiced
- salt and freshly ground black pepper to taste

Directions

- Stir fry your garlic for 6 mins in olive oil then add your leeks and continue cooking for it 11 mins.
- Now top the mix with pepper, lemon juice, and salt.
- Let the contents gently cook with a low to medium level of heat for 17 more mins.
- Enjoy.

Amount per serving (8 total)

Timing Information:

Preparation	15 m
Cooking	30 m
Total Time	45 m

Nutritional Information:

Calories	140 kcal
Fat	7.3 g
Carbohydrates	18g
Protein	1.8 g
Cholesterol	0 mg
Sodium	23 mg

* Percent Daily Values are based on a 2,000 calorie diet.

FRENCH TOMATO AND POTATO CASSEROLE

Ingredients

- 2 1/4 lbs potatoes, peeled and cut into chunks
- 1/2 C. heavy cream
- 3 tbsps butter
- 1 pinch ground nutmeg
- salt and pepper, to taste
- 2 tbsps olive oil
- 1 onion, diced
- 1 1/2 lbs leeks, sliced
- 2 medium tomatoes - peeled, seeded, and coarsely diced
- 1 1/2 lbs cooked ham, thinly sliced
- 1 egg yolk, lightly beaten
- 1/4 C. shredded mozzarella cheese (optional)

Directions

- Grease a baking dish with oil then set your oven to 375 degrees before doing anything else.
- Boil your potatoes in salt and water for 17 mins. Then remove all the liquid and add: pepper, cream, salt, nutmeg, and butter.
- With a masher mash these potatoes until they're smooth.
- Now begin to stir fry your onions in olive oil, until see-through, then add the leeks and cook everything for 2 more mins until the leeks are tender.
- Add the tomatoes, set the heat to low, and let the contents gently cook for 7 mins, stir the mix every two mins.
- Now add the pepper, salt, and ham.
- Continue cooking everything for 2 more mins.
- Layer your potatoes, then the ham and leeks, and then more potatoes in the baking dish.
- Then top the layers with some whisked egg yolk and cheese.

- Cook the dish in the oven for 24 mins.
- Enjoy.

Amount per serving (6 total)

Timing Information:

Preparation	15 m
Cooking	45 m
Total Time	1 h

Nutritional Information:

Calories	675 kcal
Fat	40.8 g
Carbohydrates	50.1g
Protein	28.7 g
Cholesterol	143 mg
Sodium	1572 mg

* Percent Daily Values are based on a 2,000 calorie diet.

THANKS FOR READING! NOW LET'S TRY SOME SUSHI AND DUMP DINNERS....

<u>Send the Book!</u>

To grab this **box set** simply follow the link mentioned above, or tap the book cover.

This will take you to a page where you can simply enter your email address and a PDF version of the **box set** will be emailed to you.

I hope you are ready for some serious cooking!

Send the Book!

You will also receive updates about all my new books when they are free.

Also don't forget to like and subscribe on the social networks. I love meeting my readers. Links to all my profiles are below so please click and connect :)

Facebook

Twitter

COME ON...
LET'S BE FRIENDS :)

I adore my readers and love connecting with them socially. Please follow the links below so we can connect on Facebook, Twitter, and Google+.

Facebook

Twitter

I also have a blog that I regularly update for my readers so check it out below.

My Blog

CAN I ASK A FAVOUR?

If you found this book interesting, or have otherwise found any benefit in it. Then may I ask that you post a review of it on Amazon? Nothing excites me more than new reviews, especially reviews which suggest new topics for writing. I do read all reviews and I always factor feedback into my newer works.

So if you are willing to take ten minutes to write what you sincerely thought about this book then please visit our Amazon page and post your opinions.

Again thank you!

INTERESTED IN OTHER EASY COOKBOOKS?

Everything is easy! Check out my Amazon Author page for more great cookbooks:

For a complete listing of all my books please see my author page.

Printed in Great Britain
by Amazon

33954837R00058